I0502293

EVERYTHING

N
S
D
N
S
N
D

"WAIL DICH NIER EVMIOOANE AUSTTET"

GAR GAL

I HAVE TO TO RECORD AND SEND YOU YOU N VIDES E.G. HOW I MAKE MYN INFERENT WAYS

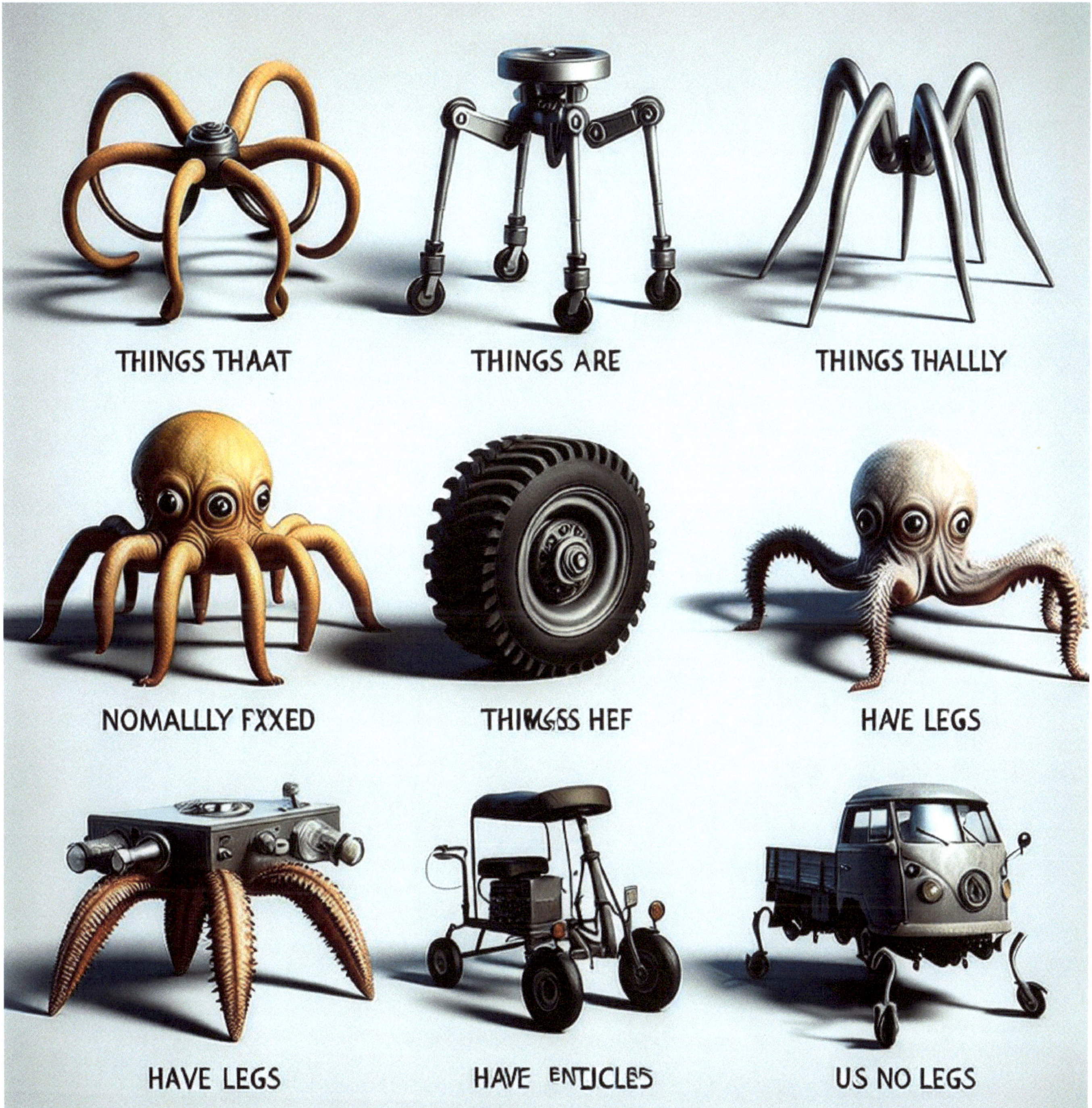
THINGS THAAT
THINGS ARE
THINGS THALLY
NOMALLLY FXXED
HAVE LEGS
HAVE LEGS
US NO LEGS

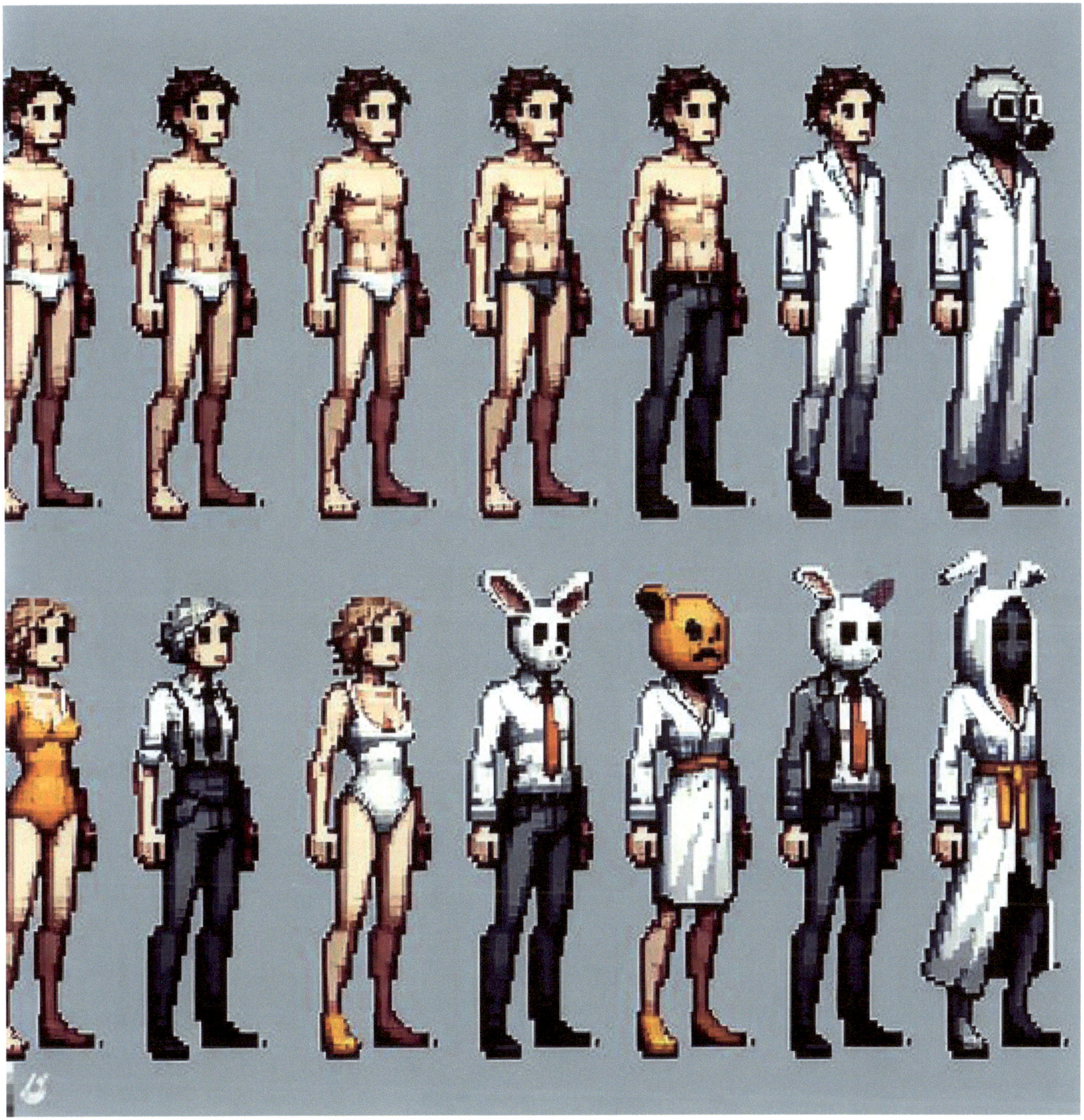

Hom,?
WHAT DIH NIEVNR NENDON AQUMET?

MOITURAREMD

How to make
you yous n im
I make yoi
diffeent ways